Pacify Your Fear

HOW TO DEAL WITH FEARS

by

ARTHUR HILL & OSWALD HOWARD

ISBN: 9798721739590

Fear: psychological foundations and scientific research of this phenomenon

Let's look at different points of view on the concept of fear:

Currently, there are many definitions of fear.
Fear is defined as a mental state that is associated with painful experiences and causes actions aimed at self-preservation.

Fear is one of the three most powerful emotions (the other two are anger and joy) and is a basic instinct.

Fear as an affective state in anticipation of any threat.

Fear is the result of suppressing an aggressive drive, which plays an important role in a person's life.

Fear is an emotion that is avoided or minimized by a person, but at the same time, fear, if manifested in a mild form, can prompt a person to learn.

Fear as a state of fear, focused on various threats that are easy to recognize, soberly analyze and adequately resist them.

Fear is a state of mind, and every person can observe it almost daily. The essence of this state is that a person is more or less aware that he is in danger.

Fear is a strong emotion experienced as anxiety or foreboding. Moreover, this is one of the most dangerous emotions that can even lead to death.

Fear was a manifestation of a natural reflex and a passive-defensive reaction based on the instinct of self-preservation.

Fear can be viewed as an emotional state that reflects the protective biological response of an individual at the moment he experiences an imaginary or real danger to well-being and health.

Fear is one of the fundamental human emotions that occurs in response to a threatening stimulus.

Fear is a very strong emotion that has a serious impact on human behavior, as well as on his perceptual and cognitive processes, limiting thinking, perception and freedom of choice.

But to one degree or another, not only the understanding of fear by various scientists and specialists is diverse, but also the approaches to its study. We definitely need to get to know them so that the phenomenon of fear becomes more understandable for us.

Directions of the study of fear

Three fundamental psychological approaches to the study of fear can be distinguished - these are psychoanalytic, behavioristic and existential approaches. Let's talk about each of them separately.

The psychoanalytic approach

As you understand, the main representative of this trend was Sigmund Freud. In his view, fear develops in close connection with the system of the unconscious and libido - the energy of mental drives. Libido turns into fear through repression - repressed sexual drives take the form of fear, and this fear is neurotic.

In studying phobias, Freud divided the neurotic process into two phases. In the first one, sexual drives are repressed and translated into fear, correlated with an external threat.In the second one, a defense system is formed that prevents a collision with this threat, and repression is an attempt by the "I" to escape from sexual desires.

In the case of other neurotic diseases, other defense systems are activated, opposing the possible development of fear.
But, be that as it may, it is the problem of fear that plays a major role in the psychology of neuroses in general.

In his work" Beyond the principle of pleasure", Freud notes that the terms "fear" and "dread" are mistakenly considered as synonymous. Distinguishing them from the standpoint of external danger, Freud says that fear, in his opinion, is a certain state of expectation of a threat or preparation for it, even if it is unknown.

Fear implies a specific object that is feared, and fear is a reflection of the moment of surprise and a state that arises in case of danger, when the individual is not prepared for it.

Freud emphasizes that the danger that serves as its basis comes from the external object, and the neurotic danger is produced by the demand of the drive. However, the demand for attraction is not something far-fetched, but quite real, and therefore neurotic fear has quite real grounds. This suggests that the relationship between neurosis and real fear is explained by the defense of the "I", because it reacts to the danger of attraction.

From the standpoint of Freud, the demand for attraction often turns into an internal danger for the reason that its satisfaction can provoke an external danger. At the same time, the real danger can become significant for the "I" only if it turns into an inner experience.

Freud says that the "I" is endangered from three sides, and it may well be seized by a threefold fear - the real fear of external reality, the fear of conscience before the "Super-I" and the neurotic fear of the "It".

Freud tried to structure the psyche, as a result of which he came to a psychoanalytic understanding of the fact that the unconscious "It" is not afraid, because it is unable to judge threat situations. Specifically, "I" serves as the focus of fear. And it is far from just that the scientist asserts that the "I" is a true hotbed of fear, and due to the presence of three dangers, it forms a "flight reflex".

 As a result, neurotic symptoms and defense mechanisms are formed, leading to the occurrence of phobias.

In the future, the American psychoanalyst Karen Horney began to develop some of Freud's ideas. In her opinion, unresolved conflicts are the cause of all fears. And in addition to this, she sees the reason in the social factors that give rise to intrapersonal conflicts, as well as in cultural values.

Behavioral approach

The founder of behaviorism, American psychologist John Watson, identified several stimuli that activate fear. These are blows and shocks at the moment of falling asleep, sudden loss of support and sudden loud noises. All other stimuli that cause fear, in his opinion, can be considered as a combination of all above mentioned. Initially, a person has unconditional, i.e. congenital fear reactions. But in the process of life, new stimuli are formed that cause fear. To prove this, Watson cited the results of his research, according to which, such things as fire, darkness, animals, etc. do not cause any fear in infancy.

As research progressed, Watson became interested, among other things, in the possibility of forming a fear response to objects that had not previously caused fear. Together with his wife Rosalia Reiner, the scientist studied the possibility of forming an emotional fear response in an 11-month-old baby. As a frightening stimulus, a white rat was taken, and earlier the baby calmly played with this rat and was with her in the crib.

Before the experiment, the boy was not afraid of rats; no deviations were observed in his development. He was also not afraid of rabbits, dogs, monkeys, or other animals. At the time of the experiment, there were three more children in the hospital, and none of them was afraid of anything like this. The experiment itself was necessary for the scientists to answer three questions:

Is it possible to instill in a baby the fear of animals if the animal is shown along with a stimulus that causes fear?

Will the child be afraid of other animals as well?

How long will acquired fear last?

The stimulus causing fear in the experiment was a loud sound - behind the baby's back, scientists pounded on an iron plate with a hammer.
 During the first session, the plate was hit twice each time the child touched the white rat. And after two repetitions, the baby began to avoid touching the rat.

The experiment was repeated a week later. The plate had already been beaten five times, and the rat was simply placed in the baby's crib. The kid showed a reaction of avoidance and began to cry as soon as he saw a rat. And five days later, scientists decided to test whether the fear reaction would carry over to other objects.

As a result, Watson noted the child's fear at the sight of a dog, a rabbit and a fur coat. Also, the child tried not to come into contact with the Santa Claus mask and ordinary cotton wool. Considering that there were no loud sounds when demonstrating these objects, the scientist decided that the reaction was carried over to objects similar to a white rat.

As a result, Watson drew analogies and concluded that many fears, anxiety states and antipathies in adults are formed in the first years of life. A little later, the researcher found that acquired fears are characterized by high resilience, ease of transferring to similar situations and stimuli. And to eliminate fears, long-term therapy is necessary, however, only one fear can be weakened, and the reaction to adjacent situations and stimuli remain the same.

Another scientist who applied a behavioral approach to the study of fears was the American psychologist Burrès Frederick Skinner, who developed the theory (model) of operant conditioning of fears. The essence of this model is that fear can be generated, maintained, and reinforced by the reinforcement that occurs after the fearful behavior. Reinforcement can be both positive and negative.

Positive reinforcement can be illustrated as follows: a child can get scared of something and run to his parents to protect him, and they give him protection, affection and care. Subsequently, in any similar situation, the child increasingly begins to turn to his parents, thereby applying a strategy of escape from the frightening stimulus.

In some cases, the child may even resort to feigning fear to get reinforcement again. In this case, fear has a so-called hidden benefit. And most of all, such fears are fixed if fear for the child is the only opportunity to receive parental attention.

Given that fear is a negative stimulus, anyone will seek to prevent it. And every time it succeeds, there is negative reinforcement. As a result, the fear is reinforced by itself. This can explain that fear is very difficult to suppress, even if there is no conditioned stimulus.

If you are interested in the ideas of behaviorists, you can also pay attention to the work of other representatives of this area of psychology - E. Thorndike, W. Hunter, K. Lashley, A. Staats. By the way, read our article "Behaviorism: Fundamentals, Representatives and Directions", and we go further.

The existential approach

The existential approach, also called existential logotherapy, was proposed by the Austrian psychiatrist and psychologist Viktor Frankl. He presented the mechanism of the formation of the fear reaction as follows: a person is afraid of some phenomenon and an expectation reaction appears, i.e. fear that this phenomenon is being realized.

Further, symptoms of the expected condition may appear, due to which the fear increases. Thus, the chain of tension is closed: the fear of anticipating danger becomes stronger than the fears associated with the danger directly. And a person begins to react to this fear by withdrawing from reality.

Fear often appears when something related to it happens, when a person experiences appropriate experiences.
For example, a person is about to speak in public, he is worried and notices that he is "shaken". When he has to perform again, the person's excitement begins to be supplemented by the fear that he will start to shake again, and, of course, this is what happens.

As a result, a person begins to avoid speaking in public, because he thinks that he will be shaken again and he will not be able to suppress and hide it.

And if the fear is not overcome in a timely manner, the situation can get worse. Thus, a phobia develops, leading to a constant recurrence of symptoms, as a result of which the initial fears become stronger.

Based on this, Frankl proposed to apply self-alienation, the ability to which is most clearly manifested in humor. With the help of humor, a person can distance himself from absolutely everything, including himself and his experiences, which means he is able to begin to control himself and the situation.

According to Frankl, fear is a biological response that avoids real or perceived danger situations. And if a person himself begins to actively look for situations of fear, he will learn to act, bypassing fear, which will make the latter disappear. "Atrophies" from not being "used".

Frankl has developed corrective methods for dealing with fears. One of them was the method of paradoxical intention (originally proposed by A. Adler), which assumes that the psychologist directs the "patient" to his fear. The paradox lies in the fact that a person does not run away from fear, but goes to meet it.

It is appropriate to give an interesting story here: once the parents of a 9-year-old boy turned to Frankl, who was always wetting his bed.
 No threats or punishments from the parents helped. Then the scientist made an unexpected offer to the boy: from now on, every time he wet the bed, he would give him 50 cents.

The boy was delighted and began to hope that he would be able to make money on his problem. He deliberately began to do everything he could to make the bed wet, but nothing came of it. As a result, the neurotic symptom disappeared, and it disappeared at the very moment when the desire to repeat this symptom began to prevail in the child's mind.

Frankl suggested doing the same with other fears: if a person is afraid of confined spaces, he must force himself to be in such a space; if he is afraid of frogs, he must force himself to pick up and hold the frog, etc. And with a long and / or systematic appeal of a person to his fear, he will be able to successfully overcome it.

These are the main ideas of Viktor Frankl. If you want to get to know them better, you should study the work of this person. And besides the three considered approaches, two more can be distinguished:

Sensual approach

A person's assessment of a situation of fear is based on feelings.

Cognitive approach

A person's idea of fear is formed on the basis of intellectual processes.

The psychoanalytic approach says that the nature of fear is intimately connected with the system of the unconscious;

The behavioral approach considers fear as a complex of reactions that arise in response to external stimuli;
The existential approach interprets fear as a phenomenon that occurs at the earliest stage of human development.

The problem of fear, despite the fact that it has its roots in the distant past, remains relevant even in our time, because such a phenomenon as fear will exist as long as the person himself exists. Along with the development of society, fear will acquire new forms. People will create new ways to work with fear.

Fear is designed to activate a person's strength or stop him in moments of danger. But fear also has a number of negative qualities, directing a person's actions in a completely sub-optimal, and sometimes even destructive channel.

Fear refers to the basic emotions of a person, and they are known to have a powerful effect on all aspects and aspects of his life. Being formed at the early stages of human development, fear subsequently accompanies him throughout his life, being an integral part of it.

We feel fear in a wide variety of situations, but they all have one thing in common - we perceive and feel them when the well-being, tranquility, safety and life of ourselves or our loved ones are threatened. Fear also participates in the social development of the individual, and fear acts as a kind of means of education, because it often regulates behavior.

Typology of fears. The most common fears and phobias

Regardless of whether the fear is rational or irrational, you need to understand it in order to determine your further actions and generally be able to assess your state. Therefore, it is necessary to learn the main features of fear. Next, we will tell you about what forms of fear exist, and introduce you to the most common types.

Forms of fears

Fears can be classified according to various criteria. We will talk about some of them below, but for now we will consider the classification of emotional states, one way or another associated with fear, based on the intensity, objectivity and strength of perception. Everything is extremely simple here, because you yourself are not by hearsay familiar with such things as:

Calmness
A state of complete emotional peace, when a person is not disturbed by anything, he is psychologically comfortable, he does not experience any negatively colored states associated with fear.

Anxiety (apprehension, worry)
 The state in which a person feels the uncertainty of the situation, expects a bad turn of events. Most often, anxiety has no objective stimulus and is irrational.

Excitement
A condition arising from anxiety and representing an intensified form of it. With it, a person experiences a more intense nervous excitement, because he does not know what could happen to him, and is afraid of it.

Fear
A condition caused by a real or perceived threat. Let us recall that there is a healthy fear that warns against danger, and there is an unhealthy fear that has no foundation. It is with him that you need to be able to cope.

Horror
A condition generated by intense fear. It can plunge a person into numbness, trembling, shock. There is no active reaction of a person with horror; he cannot eliminate the source of fear.

Panic
A state that is another extreme form of fear, but it is expressed not in numbness, but in the fact that a person begins to be controlled by his feelings. At the same time, his actions are not subject to any logic and often harm him.

We can also highlight another state associated with fear. This is a state of fearlessness. In the case of a real threat, it can lead to extremely sad consequences. You can observe the state of fearlessness in people with a hypertrophied and unhealthy sense of self-confidence, people who do not have a sense of self-preservation and suffer from mental disabilities (we are not talking about situations when circumstances require fearlessness).

But this is only an initial classification of fears, giving a general idea of how fear can be expressed in general.

Spatial fears (this includes bathophobia - fear of depth, acrophobia - fear of heights, agoraphobia - fear of open space,claustrophobia - fear of enclosed space, etc.)
Social fears (this includes neophobia - fear of any change, heterophobia - fear of the opposite sex, etc.) p.)
Fear of illness
Fear of death
Fear of sex
Fear of harming others
Fear of fears (this fear, by the way, is the cause of all phobias)
Real fears
Neurotic fears
Constructive fears
Pathological fears

Natural fears
This includes everything that is justified by natural phenomena (hurricanes, earthquakes, tsunamis, thunderstorms, etc.) Such fears are fully justified and even adequate people are subject to them. It is in human nature itself to be afraid of everything unknown.

Despite the fact that today a person perfectly understands the origin of most natural phenomena, fear of them remains, and it is natural. The fear of various animals, insects and other living beings can be attributed to the same category of fears.

Social fears
Taking the results of various sociological polls as a basis, we came to the conclusion that the greatest fear among people is, of course, the threat of war. And this fear is inherent even to those who have never participated in hostilities. Among other social fears, we can name fear of crime, hooliganism and disorder, fear for their loved

ones, fear of death, fear of poverty, fear of public speaking and publicity in general, fear of change and some others.

Internal fears

In childhood many of us were frightened. We grew up, but the fear of looking in the mirror at night, looking under the bed or pulling a leg out from under the covers remained with many.

A person's fantasy, which received a corresponding message in childhood, is capable of giving rise to a variety of monsters. And to stop being afraid of such things is very, very difficult (by the way, read our article "What were famous people afraid of", where there is a lot of confirmation of what was said).

The line between these three groups of fears is very thin and extremely difficult to see. For example, if a person experiences an inner fear of a quagmire that sucks him in, it can, to a certain extent, be attributed to both social and natural fear. Fears can be cunningly each other intertwined with and have an inexplicable effect on a person.

But this is not the end of the classification of fears, because there is also their gradation by age:

Children's fears

When a child is just beginning to live, he has a gene pool of reflexes. For example, a toddler may fear being thrown up when he hears loud noises or sees strangers. These reactions are normal and constructive, but life goes on. If the parental upbringing was incorrect or the child was influenced by some special circumstances, he may develop neurotic fears.

 For example, if a child is punished by being locked in a closet, he may develop claustrophobia, and if his mother once lost him in a shopping center, he may become afraid of open spaces and large crowds

Fears of an adult

An adequate adult understands perfectly well that there is no Boogeyman in a dark closet, but he can be horrified by one species of snakes, spiders or praying mantises. In the same way, he may be afraid that a loved one will leave him, or be afraid of the stage; to be afraid of being worse than others or to consider oneself unworthy of many benefits; overly control your other half or constantly worry about children, etc.

Fears of the elderly
The fears of older people can be different from those of children and adults. They are specific. Fear of the dark, mice and hurricanes can be added to the fear of getting sick and becoming a burden to your family. But at the same time, fears that previously bothered disappear, for example, the fear of being misunderstood by others, the fear of not experiencing love in life. However, some fears can go to extremes: grandmother, fearing strangers, does not even open the door to her family, grandfather, fearing transport, does not come closer than 200 meters to the road, etc.

As you know, fear can become uncontrollable and obsessive, i.e. develop into a phobia. Phobia is a manifestation of irrational fear or increased anxiety associated with real or expected objects or situations that cause fear. This is an obsessive state, aggravated in specific conditions and defying logical explanation. Under the influence of a phobia, a person is afraid and tries to avoid certain situations, activities or objects.

The most common phobias
Agoraphobia is fear of open spaces. People with this fear prefer to be indoors at all times.

Aquaphobia is a fear of water. In a hypertrophied form, it can develop into a fear of drinking even a sip of water.

Acrophobia is a fear of heights. Fear causes an ascent to any height, from a stool to mountains.

Arachnophobia is the fear of spiders. It is considered characteristic of most people in the world.

Astraphobia is a fear of thunder and lightning. A very common fear that leads people to hide in a shelter during a thunderstorm.

Aerophobia - fear of flying and aircraft. It is a hindrance for many people who want to travel.

Hemophobia is a fear of the sight of blood. At the sight of blood, even on TV, a person with such a phobia can faint.

Gerontophobia - fear of old age. Most often, this fear is observed in middle-aged people.

Homophobia is a fear, or rather rejection of homosexuality and people with non-traditional sexual orientation.

Dentophobia is a fear of dentists. People with this phobia would prefer to endure acute toothache rather than sit in a dentist's chair.
Kakorrhaphiophobia - fear of failure. It is characteristic mainly of people who are focused exclusively on success.

Kinophobia is a fear of dogs. Another type of phobias inherent in a huge number of people.

Claustrophobia is a fear of confined spaces. A person with an aggravated form of this phobia begins to panic in a regular elevator.

Xenophobia is the fear of strangers. Can develop in sexual, interracial and religious grounds.

Monophobia is the fear of being alone. It can be expressed in the form of fear of being abandoned by a loved one, being alone in the world, or being alone in a room.

Necrophobia is the fear of the dead. A striking example of fear of the unknown.

Nobodyphobia is fear of the dark. Despite the fact that it affects mainly children, it is also noted in a huge number of adults.

Ophidiophobia is the fear of snakes. Another example of a common fear. It is a subspecies of gipert phobia - fear of reptiles.

Social phobia is the fear of public attention. This can even include the fear of appearing in public places.

Thanatophobia - fear of death. This fear paralyzes a person's will and prevents him from living a normal life.

Trypanophobia is a fear of needles, injections and injections. The usual vaccination becomes a test of strength for people with this phobia.

Trypophobia is a fear of open wounds and any holes in the skin - both on one's own and on the skin of any living organism in general.

Or here are some of the strangest phobias found in the modern world:

Agmenophobia - the fear that a person's queue will advance more slowly than the next one;

Acrophobia - fear of not understanding the essence of what you read;

Haptophobia - fear of touching;

Hexakosioihexekontahexaphobia - fear of the number "666";

Genophobia - fear of intimacy;

Hippopotomonstrosesquippedaliophobia - fear of long words;

Dextrophobia - fear of objects located on the right;

Decidophobia - fear of decision making;

Domatophobia - fear of houses and any buildings;

Barophobia - fear of giving and receiving gifts;

Ignorophobia - fear of not receiving a response to a read message;

Emoji Phobia - afraid to be misunderstood after sending a smiley or a sticker;

Cyberphobia - fear of computers;

Koumpounophobia - fear of buttons;

Lachanophobia - fear of vegetables;

Macrophobia - fear of long waiting;

Neophobia - fear of clouds;

Nomophobia - fear of being without a smartphone;

Omphalophobia - fear of navels;

Papaphobia - fear of the Pope;

Pentheraphobia - fear of mother-in-law;

Pogonophobia - afraid of beards;

Punctum Phobia - afraid of messages with a dot at the end;

Retrophobia - fear of making a mistake in a word or not seeing an erroneous autocorrect;

Self Phobia - fear of taking a low-quality selfie;

Socionethobia - fear of social networks;

Philophobia - fear of falling in love;

Hydrophobia - fear of laughing in inappropriate conditions;

Chorophobia - fear of dancing;

Chronophobia - fear of time;

Epistemophobia - fear of gaining knowledge;

Ergophobia - fear of any job.

And this list of phobias by no means exhausts the topic, which suggests that it is possible, perhaps, to find any fear, even in a mild form, in any person in the world. Moreover, with the passage of time and the change in the specifics of each era, new, sometimes completely absurd fears appear.

Fear. What to do with it ?

Did you know, for example, that 15 to 20 percent of all people experience phobias, and about 9% of Americans over the age of 18 have at least one specific fear? [Diagnostic and Statistical Manual of Mental Disorders, American Psychiatric Association Text Edition Fourth Edition].

Generally speaking, the results of research by Chapman University [America's Top Fears, 2015] showed that 90% of all people in the world in general experience fear from time to time, and 40% of them face problems because of this fear. And the problems, in turn, can be very different, from mild psychological discomfort to depression and self-restraint, inability to achieve success in life and become happy, serious mental illnesses and even suicide.

Naturally, we are not talking about the fact that such by no means bright prospects await everyone. But in any case, if there is a desire to live a full life, expand your boundaries and develop, fears must be worked through.

What is fear? Why is it needed? Does it help or harm?

Fear is a state of nervous excitement, which is characterized by the experience of a sense of danger or threat. It is one of the very first feelings experienced by a person in life, and it accompanies a person throughout his life path. Fear is one of the basic emotions, and this emotion is designed to protect a person in case of danger and uncertainty.

Fear was still characteristic of primitive man, and when he encountered some natural phenomenon or a ferocious animal, it was fear that made him run away, seek shelter or engage in battle in order to save his life.

But we live in a modern world, the main function of fear in which itself has receded into the background. Today we no longer need to hide from a thunderstorm, throw a spear at a mammoth, or flee from a saber-toothed tiger. However, fear takes a variety of forms, and in some cases it certainly helps, but in other situations it does not play into our hands.

What is the use of fear?

Fear can serve for the benefit of a person, but only when it is directly related to the situation and proportionate to its scale, i.e. not exaggerated. In such cases, it would be much worse if there was no fear, because if we feel danger, it makes us think whether it is worth taking this or that step.

The functions of the body are mobilized, and as a result we are ready for an unforeseen development of events. At some point, we find ourselves paralyzed, as it were, and this allows us to orient ourselves, think over actions, calculate forces and decide what to do next: run, hide, resist something.

Hence the conclusion that fear does not need to be drowned out. On the contrary, it should be listened to in order to cope with extreme situations. And another plus of fear is that it reminds us that life goes by and will end someday. This motivates us to live it more consciously and fully, makes us not put off important things for later.

Fear also contributes to self-knowledge. It seems to say that we are responsible for everything that happens to us, indicates that our life is fragile, and therefore we should rely only on ourselves and our strength. We ourselves are the smiths of our own happiness and we ourselves are obliged to take an active part in our lives. But what is the other side of the coin?

What is the harm of fear?

When fear turns out to be far-fetched and has little to do with reality, when the threat is imaginary and there is simply no reason for it, fear has a destructive effect on a person.

It can cause relative harm - to restrict a person's freedom, make him passive, distort and even narrow his perception of what is happening. And if this fear arises over and over again, it becomes impossible to live a full life.

And unreasonable fear can cause absolute harm, becoming a serious psychological hindrance in life. We lose the opportunity to realize our potential, to do what we like and want. And just with such fears (by the way, you can read about the types of fears and phobias in a separate article "Types of Fears") and you need to learn to fight.

What is the point of dealing with fear?

Surely you yourself have already concluded that living without fear, of course, is impossible. If it were not, we would cease to feel dangers and threats, we would not be afraid of anything, which means that we would underestimate the real world, which can be very unpredictable. The result of all this would be at least serious troubles, and as a maximum - death.

So why should we fight fear? In fact, everything is very simple: if you do not take into account the fear that saves us from real danger and death, but consider only those fears and phobias that interfere with life (fear of public speaking, fear of success, fear of closeness with people, etc. .), fighting them will automatically make our life better.

Overcoming ourselves and ceasing to be afraid of something, we become stronger as individuals, reveal internal reserves, expand the comfort zone, develop intelligence, gain a lot of useful knowledge and skills, as well as a huge number of opportunities that were not there before.

A trivial example: you have always dreamed of becoming an orator, and since childhood you have fantasized about performing in front of a huge audience, talking about something important and interesting for you and the public. But here's the bad luck: you are seized with horror and panic when at least five people are looking at you at the same time. As a result, you cannot fulfill your dream, do what your heart is about.

Start working with this fear. Even if not immediately, but after a while you will cease to be afraid to be in sight of people and will be able to gradually begin to master the basics of oratory. And if you continue, your dream will turn into a real goal that you can quite fulfill yourself.

And there are many such examples. But the most interesting thing is that the principles of dealing with fears in most cases are the same. It is enough to learn a few rules and techniques, and your life will begin to transform. And the first step towards getting rid of fears is to understand their causes.

Where do fears come from?

The sooner we find out the cause of this or that fear, the sooner we get rid of it. One of the most authoritative researchers of fear, the American psychologist Sylvan Solomon Tomkins, in his studies [Tomkins, 1962-1963] names drives, emotions and cognitive processes as the causes of fear.

Drive is an instinctive desire, and it acquires psychological significance when its intensity reaches a critical point. The human brain receives a signal about an acute physiological deficit, which activates the emotion of fear.

Fear can be activated by any emotion - this is where the principle of emotional contamination comes into play. For example, the reaction of fear and arousal, due to the fact that its neurophysiological mechanisms are similar to the mechanisms on which the emotion of fear is based, can activate this fear.

Also, fear can act as a cognitive assessment of the situation. For example, it can be triggered by a mental image or memory. By the way, most often it is cognitive processes that serve as a reflection of fictitious rather than real situations, as a result of which a person begins to fear that he does not actually carry any threat.

Another famous scientist, psychiatrist John Bowlby, in his work [Bowlby, 1969] points out a role in the activation of fear in biology. He calls it the causes of such natural danger signals as a sharp approach of an object, sudden noise or pain. He also says that fear can appear if a person is suddenly reminded of past experiences or serious mistakes.

Here are some more scientific facts: Austrian psychiatrist and psychologist Sigmund Freud insisted that both childhood and adult fears stem from an unused libido. This energy of psychic drives, if not used, is transformed into fear.

Scientists also believed that the main cause of fear is physiological mechanisms, reflex reactions to external and internal stimuli, disturbances in the processes of self-regulation of the functional state of the brain.

In their works, you can also find references to the fact that the factor predisposing for the appearance of fear is the weakness of the nervous processes, changes in living conditions, changes in activity.

Psychologist Fritz Riemann pays special attention among the factors influencing the emergence of fears to the individual characteristics of a person: heredity, predisposition, individual living conditions, the history of the development and formation of the individual.

The reasons why we experience certain fears depend on the individual characteristics of each of us: gender, age, character and temperament, social environment. And conditionally fears, based on reasons, can be divided into several groups:

Inborn fears are fears associated with the collective unconscious and conditioned by the instinct of self-preservation. The reasons for these fears lie in the subconscious of each of us, and it is very difficult to eliminate them.

Acquired fears are fears caused by some events in the past, for example, strong feelings, fear, painful experiences, etc. These fears are quite amenable to elaboration.

Imaginary fears are fears associated with something that a person has never experienced. The reasons for such fears are people's stories, media reports, outside influence. Such fears are relatively easy to deal with.

We can also highlight hidden and obvious reasons for fears. A person can remember, know and be aware of obvious reasons, which means that it is easiest to eliminate them. And with hidden causes, things are more complicated, and most often they stem from childhood.

Such reasons include increased parental care or painful attachment to parents, all sorts of temptations, unmet needs, the consequences of psychological trauma, unresolved problems, intrapersonal conflicts, etc.

Another category of causes is cognitively engineered. These include such things as a feeling of loneliness, a feeling of rejection, depression, a threat to self-expression, the impossibility of self-realization, a feeling of one's own inferiority or even inadequacy, a feeling of approaching something bad, negative thinking.

All of the above indicates that understanding and eliminating the causes of fears, as well as eliminating fear itself, is a necessary condition for maintaining a person's mental health and the formation of psychological stability.

Undoubtedly, we all need fear, but only the kind of fear that is the basis of our well-being. Any other fears and phobias have an extremely negative effect on life and personality, and there is no doubt that they need to be dealt with.

How to deal with fears?

Learn more about what you are afraid of.
What helps a person overcome fear? Information about it. For example, the fear of childbirth prevalent among women is usually caused by the dramatic stories of more experienced girlfriends and the dominance of myths associated with this topic.

Therefore, a very important stage in preparing for the birth of a child is attending special courses for pregnant women. In the classroom, explanatory conversations about the clinical course of childbirth are conducted and a positive psychological attitude is formed: "at the finish line, the main prize awaits you."

This rational approach applies to other fears as well. Afraid to fly? It's time to get acquainted with how the plane works, where the very "strange" sounds that usually plunge into panic come from, what the turbulence zone is and what situations can really happen on board the airliner. And for a complete immersion in the topic, you can go on an excursion to the aviation training center.

Knowledge is the main force in the fight against fear, especially if it is backed up by action.

Wedge

Yes, this method also helps to cope with your fear. Deliberately immersing a person in a confusing context is useful even in the case of severe anxiety disorders. This method is rooted in Pavlov's conditioned reflex theory, which views phobia as a response to a threatening stimulus.

Therefore, in order for the extinction of this reaction to occur, it is necessary to constantly, but gradually collide the fearful person with the object of his phobia. Of course, this does not guarantee that a person will completely get rid of his fear, but it will allow him to react less emotionally and make adequate decisions in similar circumstances.

Remember, the sooner you start to face your fear, the easier it will be to overcome it. Every frightening situation reinforces fear. It is best to knock out fear in the first week after its formation.

Understand your fear

How to work through fear correctly? For example, a person is afraid to meet girls. You can, of course, try to jump into a relationship and start getting to know everyone. It is good if a person immediately starts to succeed somehow and he receives positive reinforcement. And if not? And most likely not, because fear fetters, it is unlikely to be natural and hold on well. Then it turns out that fear only gets stronger.

Try to be in your fear. If you look at fear metaphorically, it's a tin can tied to a puppy's tail. The puppy runs, the can knocks, rattles, and he is afraid of this. He starts to run even faster, but the can only rumbles more from this. This will not solve the problem, you will not run away from fear.

What should be done? First of all, you need to stop and decide to look at your fear. What are you afraid of? What scares you now?

Returning to the fear of dating a girl. Try to admit to yourself what exactly scares you. The process itself or the consequences, or maybe all of the above. Often a person is afraid of both. That he will not be good enough, somehow not so perceived, will not be able to cheer and interest the girl. As a result, she will not want to continue the relationship. But, if you don't try, then there won't be any relationship.

Stay alone with your fear, try to look into it. Maybe even strengthen it somehow. Imagine this situation, find yourself in it and look around, try to settle down in it. And when this happens, you will probably understand that there is nothing to be afraid of.

Probably everyone has such experience. For example, children are afraid of the dark; for many, this fear disappears with age. How do they overcome it? They do not fight it in any way and do not run away from it. It's just that at some point they remain with darkness and they are in it. As a result, the anxious feeling goes away, because fear is something that exists only in our head, but not in reality.

Just don't confuse a sense of danger with imaginary fears. For example, if 3 broad-shouldered guys came up to you at night and demanded a wallet, and you got scared. This is normal. This is a real threat to life, the instinct of self-preservation works.

It's another matter if you are sitting at home and are afraid to go out, because suddenly 3 hefty guys will come up to you. This fear is formed in your head. Stay with your fear, think about where it originates from. Why do you think it will happen this way?

Second step

This was the first step. When a person remains a little with his fear, the latter begins to retreat, because the person begins to understand that this is unreality. There is courage or readiness to take the next step - an experiment.

Returning to the first example, the experiment is an attempt to talk to a girl, it is not necessary to get acquainted. It is very important to do this while remaining considerate of yourself. Feel how fear rages inside, thoughts appear: you are talking some nonsense, you are not behaving like that, you do not look like that. And the reaction of the other person will help us to see that this has nothing to do with reality.

The more a person is able to carry out such experiments, the more clearly the true picture will emerge: no one reacts to us like that.

Legalize your fear

There is another technique that can help a person alleviate the situation - to legitimize your fear. If you are afraid, nervous, but still ready to talk to a girl or a guy (there is no difference), admit to your interlocutor that you are worried.

Once you have legitimized your fear, you have absolve yourself of responsibility for it. When a person himself admits that he is going through, he ceases to be nervous about the fact that it will be noticeable. One feels a kind of relief, since there is one less thought process.

Playing Tetris
According to experts, psychotherapeutic treatment of anxiety disorders should ideally be combined with relaxation techniques such as mindful breathing, meditation and yoga.

There is another non-standard way to distract from pressing fears offered at Oxford. This is a Tetris game. Scientists have found that in the process of folding the falling cubes, people's memories of negative events are modified.

Listing Items
Try listing the items you see for a minute. In the process, you will start adding additional words. In this exercise, the brain switches from emotion to logical reasoning (designation of objects), blood flows from the right hemisphere to the left, and you calm down.

If you practice this way during the week, then at the right moment 2-3 seconds will be enough for you to switch.

How to train? In your free time, it is enough to name 15-20 items (about 1 minute). There is no need to count, only to list.

Breathing technique
This and the previous method cannot completely eliminate fear. With the help of them, you can only weaken this feeling at the right time.

Take a half-breath, then exhale slowly, fully. Don't breathe for 2 seconds. Then repeat these steps until you feel your heart start to slow down. This exercise deprives the brain of oxygen and allows you to calm down.

A visit to a psychologist
How does a psychologist help in the fight against fear? It helps a person to start taking the first steps, to look at their fear. Often a person is afraid to ask himself questions, to face his fear. This is not easy to do.

It is much easier for an outside psychologist to investigate this fear. He may ask something completely banal:

what are you afraid of;
what exactly scares you;
what will happen if this happens.

The psychologist helps the person begin the process of exploring their own fear. And this is the first step - the most difficult and most important in this work.

Further, when a person begins to explore his own fear, he begins to move. The psychologist can accompany him in this process, help him integrate his new experience, show the other side, which the person in fear does not notice. Since gradually, step by step, a person begins to get rid of fear.

How fear works

In an emergency, the human brain engages three key areas. First, there is a reaction from the amygdala. It is a region in the human brain that is responsible for emotional responses in general and for the generation of fear in particular. The amygdala speeds up breathing and pulse, prepares a person for action.

Next, the hippocampus, the memory store, is connected, and the prefrontal cortex, the analytical center of the brain. All of these areas help to correctly explain the situation of concern. For example, when you observe a lion in a zoo, the first reaction is from the amygdala - to run as far as possible. But then the prefrontal cortex helps to understand that the lion is in a cage and there is nothing to be afraid of.

What conclusion can be drawn? In order for a person to eventually make the right decision, the "thinking" brain must give feedback to the "emotional" brain.

Overcoming the initial "fight or flight" impulse through the realization that the threat is unreality gives the person a sense of security and satisfaction. This is why many people love horror movies. But not all.

Why we fear without cause

Some people are unable to slow down the vigorous activity of their amygdala (amygdala), so they take horror films and literature too close to their hearts, as if they are really threatened in real life.

The same feeling is experienced by someone with a phobia or post-traumatic stress disorder. Uncontrolled fear "overexcited" his amygdala, putting the body in a state of stress and preventing the prefrontal cortex from assessing the situation soberly.

Deep-rooted negative memories of past experiences play a crucial role in the emergence of this irrational fear. So, a survivor of a car accident shudders for a long time even from a simple squeal of brakes. Then this conditioned reaction fades away, but the memory of the initial sad event does not disappear anywhere and can again make itself felt if a similar situation arises.

Scientists have found that traumatic episodes cause long-term activation of neurons in the amygdala and hippocampus. This means that a person may have a feeling of increased anxiety associated with the object of fear for a long time, depriving him of the opportunity to function normally and enjoy life.

No need to suppress fear

Do not try to directly suppress obsessive fear in a person, especially when it comes to the so-called "justified" fear that has developed on the basis of severe physical or psychological trauma. In the case of irrational fear, such a technique will also not work, but rather will lead to the opposite result. It is important to work through the fear correctly.

How anxious expectation works

Most of all in a dangerous situation, many are worried about the uncertainty of the future, which, by the way, is skillfully used by the creators of horror films.

The state of anxious expectation heightens the sense of impending threat, which in turn can influence the subjective perception of time and pain. And it's scientifically proven! For example, it seems to novice skydivers that the wait before jumping out of the plane lasts endlessly, although in reality it takes only a few minutes.

This phenomenon is familiar to everyone to one degree or another. Think about how you "wind up" yourself on the eve of an important interview or in line to the dentist.

Don't beat yourself up. "Anxiety of expectation" is a normal reaction of the body that helps to "get together", and it should be regulated only if it becomes destructive.

The best way to calm fear is a sense of control over a situation. And control is achieved through awareness.

What are inflated fears and how to confront them

Many modern fears are regularly fueled by the media and the Internet, which can lead to "social panic". As a rule, this panic does not correspond to the real threat.

"A typical example: for some reason people are afraid of contracting the Zika or Ebola virus, although the same influenza virus is statistically more likely and also dangerous. Millions die every year from it, but we still do not take it seriously, but we extol "exotic" infections and fear them.

This state of affairs is directly related to the activities of the media, which shape public opinion, but are not always able to understand the issue.

The same applies to the fear of gluten, genetically modified foods and vaccinations: a "reason" appears in the information space, and then people pick it up and begin to speculate on it.

The problem of "inflated fears" is very acute, and perhaps the only way to combat this phenomenon is education. Then there is a chance that these fears will disappear into oblivion, as in due time the fear of witches, red women and black cats.

Conclusion

Everyone has to deal with a frightening situation at least once in their life. You can get scared and run away. Or fight. Or withdraw into yourself for a while and rethink everything thoroughly. Everyone makes their own choice. There is no perfect recipe for dealing with fear.

The main thing is to do something. If you continue to work with your fear, do something and observe it, it starts to recede. You become freer.

Awareness of your fear

The technique of overcoming fear is based on careful planning. Only knowing how to act in the event of anxiety, phobias and other negative manifestations, you can move on. In addition, a person must understand that the struggle with their own fears is work. It will take a lot of effort to win over yourself. And this is not easy.

Overcoming the fear of public speaking

It should also be understood that learning to coexist with such an emotion is a vital task for a person. Absolute fearlessness leads to destruction. Therefore, you need to treat fear with respect. This is an important emotion that has gone through a long evolutionary path with humanity.

It is necessary to start the fight against negative manifestations of fear with introspection. This will increase the level of personal comfort. You need to look at yourself from the outside. So, for example, overcoming fear of public speaking begins with studying the reasons that cause it. A person must understand exactly what situations he is afraid of. He is afraid to seem stupid in the eyes of the audience, uninteresting, his opinion will not be heard, etc. You also need to understand what we should be in order for the situation to become favorable.

This approach allows you to develop a strategy of behavior. There are a number of fears that need to be consciously resisted.

An important point in the process of creating a strategy is the awareness of your fear. It must be admitted. It should be understood that by experiencing fear, you do not become worse, weaker. Every person experiences similar emotions. This does not mean at all that you are weak or less respected. There are many people out there who experience the exact same fear. If you ignore it, this does not mean that negative emotions will disappear. They are rather aggravated. Admitting your fear is the first step towards controlling it.

Rationalization, Observation

Overcoming the fear of death, fire, water, lack of money, etc. must begin with the process of rationalization. It is worth looking at the situation correctly. Of course, everyone is afraid to die. This is facilitated by our survival instinct. This fear is understandable. But being afraid to die every time you go out is illogical. In such cases, you need to remember about the probability with which such an event can occur. If there is no war outside the window, stones do not fall from the sky, the probability of perishing is small. Especially if a person looks around, avoids knowingly dangerous situations (for example, crossing the road at a red light).

You should definitely look at your fears rationally. This allows you to gain control over them.

Overcoming your fear of speaking should start with observing other people. Don't think that you are alone in your feelings. A huge number of people are afraid of this. The difference can only be in the degree of intensity of an atypical emotion. However, all people get nervous before going on stage. Especially if you need to perform alone, without a team. Watching how other people deal with this unpleasant feeling can help you overcome your own fear.

Improving self-esteem

Another effective technique for overcoming fear is to deliberately increase self-esteem. If a person has a fear of communication, he may catch himself on certain negative thoughts about himself. Unable to overcome the barrier,in order to approach a person to start a conversation, we tend to reproach ourselves, saying phrases in our head, for example, "I'm a loser," "I'm a weakling," "no one needs such a weak person like me." Such thoughts have an extremely negative impact on our perception of ourselves.

You should cheer yourself up. It is necessary to mentally pronounce: "Although it is difficult for me now to overcome this barrier, to start a conversation, I can do it. I am an interesting conversationalist. People strive to communicate with me. " Even if it is not possible to decide on a conversation the first time, over time, a person will be able to step over his fear. This feeling is like jumping from a tower. Looking down into the water, a person is afraid to jump. However, in flight, he already forgets about his fear. It is the same with other fears. The fear is much greater until the moment when the person decides to take action.

Relaxation techniques and challenge yourself

There are special exercises for overcoming fears. A person must learn to accept negative emotion. It is necessary to face it. If a person is afraid to even think about his fear, he aggravates the situation. You can't run from him. You need to accept that there are certain situations that are scary. For example, it could be a plane ride. This will prevent travel to other countries. A person loses certain opportunities. You need to come to terms with the idea that sooner or later you will have to fly by plane.

Ways to overcome fears

A good exercise in this case is the relaxation technique. If a wave of anxiety, panic rushes over, you need to calm down, concentrating on your breathing. It should be measured, even. A few minutes after breathing exercises, mental balance is restored. A person will be able to think soberly by taking control of the situation. You can also count in your mind. The numbers are spoken slowly. Simple exercises can help you get rid of your fear.

Another technique that allows you to overcome fears is challenging yourself. A person must understand what he is afraid of. By visualizing your fear, you can challenge it, start a fight with it, as with the worst enemy. If you are afraid of an action, you need to perform it. It will be pretty hard. However, over time, a person will be able to completely overcome the unpleasant feeling in himself. For example, if there is a fear of spiders, you need to start small. First you just need to go into the room that contains this insect. When a person can enter the room, he has already partially overcome his fear.

Then, after a while, you need to pull yourself together and approach the spider. You can consider it. This procedure is performed until the fear disappears completely. After that, the most difficult thing follows - you need to take the spider in your hand. To do this, you can ask loved ones to help in a similar matter. A person is blindfolded, and someone close to him holds a model of a spider in his hand. At the same time, a person must imagine how he approaches a spider, and then takes it in his hand. After such training, you can approach a real spider. After that, you will be able to cope with the fear.

Fight fear gradually

Experts say that methods of overcoming fear are based on a gradual problem solving. In other words, if a person is afraid of drowning, you cannot push him off the boat into the river and expect the fear to pass. It will only get worse, it will become richer. You need to move towards your goal gradually, stage by stage.

How to overcome fear in yourself?

You need to understand what result a person seeks to achieve. For example, in hot countries, contact with a spider can be really dangerous. Therefore, do not touch the insect with your hands. But in order to drive the intruder out of your home, without waiting for outside help (which may not be available at the moment), you need to force yourself to approach the insect. Then it is covered with a glass jar. Cardboard is pushed under its neck. In this state, the spider can be taken outside.

To perform such actions, a person must exercise. You need to start small. If there is a fear of swimming in the open water, you must first spend some time on the shore. When such an action does not cause fear, you can proceed with subsequent actions. They take off their shoes and walk with bare feet along the surf line. Then you can swim in shallow water. Gradually the fear recedes. Over time, a person will be able to swim a little further, where his legs do not reach the bottom.

Motivation

When studying ways to overcome fear in yourself, it is worth paying attention to such an important issue as motivation. You need to imagine how much life will change for the better when you manage to cope with your emotions. For example, a person is afraid to drive a car. He must imagine how he can go on an exciting journey in his own car if he overcomes fear.

Otherwise, a person will live with his phobia, because he will not understand why he should fight it at all. We need to clearly realize that such fears limit us, setting a certain framework. We are forced to obey them. Freedom can only be gained by conquering fear.

By considering approaches and techniques for overcoming fear, you can significantly improve the quality of your life. Anxiety and phobias will remain in the past, no longer disturbing the person.

Methods of dealing with fears and anxiety

Practically every person is able to overcome fears and anxiety, negative emotions and experiences. This is not as difficult as it might seem at first glance. You just need to set a goal and follow the advice of psychologists. So, let's take a look at the most effective professional recommendations that can be applied at home.

Identify the cause of your worries

If you want to get rid of anxiety and anxiety, be sure to find the cause. Think about the exact situation that scares you. Maybe you're afraid of heights, crowds, meeting strangers, or speaking in front of an audience. Remember when your fear first appeared, in what situation it happened.
Don't hide from your fear, don't deny it. If you honestly acknowledge its presence in your life, it will become easier to deal with it.

Learn to relax

Anxiety states force you to be in constant tension, take away energy and strength. Therefore, it is very important to learn how to relax. To do this, you can use any method: a warm bath, a walk in the park, an evening jog in the fresh air, yoga or meditation, breathing exercises, listening to pleasant, soothing music. Try to distract yourself from the worries that torment you and give yourself up to the chosen activity.

Discuss your fears with a loved one

 There is nothing better than sharing your concerns with someone you trust. This can be a close relative or friend to whom you can open your soul. Tell us what worries and worries you and listen to the opinion of the interlocutor. Very often, after such a conversation, a person begins to relate to his problem more calmly, and experiences lose their urgency.

Put your thoughts down on paper

If you don't have someone you can trust, don't despair. Keep a diary and write down any negative experiences. So it will be easier for you to understand yourself and understand what exactly worries you and in what situations fear manifests itself most strongly.

Laugh and smile often

Bring more humor into your life. Watch comedies or humorous shows, read anecdotes, search the Internet for various funny jokes. It's good to do this with friends. So you can laugh enough, relieve tension and forget about your worries for a while.

Don't sit around

When a person is not busy with anything, negative experiences begin to step on him, and dark thoughts spin in his head and do not allow him to relax. The best thing to do in a situation like this is to get busy. Do whatever you want: clean the apartment, cook a delicious dinner, pay attention to your husband or wife, play with your child, go to the store.

Give your fears and anxieties a certain amount of time. Chances are, you won't be able to keep your experiences in check all the time. You don't need to do this. Set aside 20-30 minutes for them every day. During this time, let your imagination paint the scariest pictures. Unleash your anxiety, surrender to it completely. Don't analyze your emotions, just relive them. When the allotted time is over, return to your normal activities. If anxiety begins to overwhelm you during the day, just write down the thoughts that bother you on paper, and in the allotted time you can worry.

Don't dwell on the past

If you have had unpleasant situations in the past that have caused inner fear or anxiety, your thoughts may often return to these events. Don't let them do that. The past has already passed and it is not at all a fact that the negative scenario will repeat itself again. Relax, calm your nerves and live in the moment.

Get involved in visualization

As soon as your imagination begins to paint you terrible pictures of possible events, immediately, with an effort of will, switch it into a positive direction. Provide vividly and in detail the most favorable outcome of the situation that worries you. Visualize until you feel that the anxiety has left you, or at least significantly reduced. Psychologists and esotericists argue that regular positive visualization can influence life circumstances by turning them in the desired direction.

Don't plan ahead. Usually, before an important event, people think over their every step, rehearse actions and words. If you are very anxious, then let your actions be spontaneous. Very often they turn out to be much more effective than planned.

Trust the situation and act according to the circumstances

Don't feed your fears. If you have a tendency to worry too much, try to read or watch news, crime reports, and other information on TV as little as possible that will only exacerbate existing fears and create fertile ground for new ones to emerge.

Change your eating habits

Some foods we eat tend to make anxiety worse. This includes tea, coffee, alcohol. Reduce or eliminate these foods in your diet. By the way, an excessive passion for sweets also increases anxiety, because when blood sugar rises, a person has an unreasonable feeling of anxiety.

Chat with people

If you start to feel anxious, don't sit alone. Go to a crowded place - cinema, theater, concert or exhibition. Meet with your friends often. Give preference to live communication, but if this is not possible, do not neglect talking on the phone, skype, and correspondence on the Internet.
Use affirmations, mantras, mudras. In esoteric literature, you can find many effective means to combat negative experiences. Some of the most popular are Statin's moods. You can use ready-made texts or come up with your own based on them.
Getting rid of fear: the psychology of emergence and methods of struggle

Psychologist's help in dealing with fears

If you have tried all of the above methods of dealing with anxiety, but have not achieved anything, do not get upset. It is better to seek help from a psychologist or psychotherapist.

Often, the roots of increased anxiety lie so deep in the subconscious that a person cannot find them on his own. The task of a psychologist is to help a person understand the causes of fear, remove them from the subconscious and teach him to overcome anxiety.

Some people are embarrassed to seek help from a psychologist. Do not do this. After all, you are not ashamed of a therapist or dentist, and a psychologist is the same specialist, only in the field of not physical, but mental problems. He will help you deal with your fears and provide helpful advice.

If you are having trouble dealing with your anxiety, ask your therapist to prescribe anti-anxiety medications for you. You can also use folk remedies. Drink decoctions of medicinal herbs that have a sedative effect. These include mint, lemon balm, valerian root, motherwort, chamomile.

Overcoming fears and anxieties is a step to victory

If you are tormented by anxiety or fear, do not be shy about them. Many people are afraid of something, but most of them try to overcome and remove their fears and, as a rule, they manage to win. Try it yourself.

Remember that negative emotions such as anxiety and fear can be turned into positive ones by making them work for you. Many famous people have achieved success in life precisely because of their fear, which mobilized them, forcing them to work and go to new heights.

Doctors, scientists, athletes, poets, writers, artists and representatives of many other professions were afraid to be unrecognized, they feared defeat and ridicule from other people, and these experiences helped them overcome difficulties and go to their goal, making every effort to achieve it.

As you can see, anxiety and fear can be turned from enemies into allies. Work on yourself, and you will definitely cope with your negative experiences.

Dealing with fears

In our society, it is generally accepted that fear is bad, and fear is embarrassing.

People try to overcome their fears in every possible way: when faced with the same fear periodically, they force themselves to get used to it (train themselves not to be afraid), go in for extreme sports (so that the body gets used to the adrenaline rush and in other horrible situations it would not be so scary) , hold their breath (again, so that the body gets used to the release of adrenaline and hypoxia and is more resistant to stress in anxious situations).

But which of these is really effective? How to deal with fears and is it worth fighting them?

Fear is a condition that occurs in a person when he is faced with a real threat to his life. The first and natural reaction is fading. This is the deepest and most important reaction. Freeze in order to stop and navigate the situation, to understand how to be saved. Having frozen, the person chooses the necessary tactics of behavior further. There are only three of them:

Struggle. This is the most primitive defense. If the situation requires a certain aggressiveness and a person feels the strength to fight, then he enters into a fight.

Escape. If the threat is so strong that it is pointless to fight, then the person rushes to flight.

Further freezing (torpor). In the event that a fight or flight is impossible, or the situation does not imply such modes of behavior, the organism switches to the only possible alternative of behavior - further freezing. The energy that could have received a natural discharge in the previous tactics of behavior remains inside a person, disrupting his emotional state. Some people, after a while, can still throw out these experiences, feeling helpless or experiencing outbursts of anger. For the rest, this "frozen" energy remains undischarged.

Having experienced certain traumatic events, a person intuitively begins to help himself. He avoids areas where subsequent injury could be sustained. This prevents him from being injured again, but creates chronic tension throughout the body. You must constantly be in good shape, try not to get into the same situation. At some point, the tension will make itself felt.

This may not necessarily be any disease or muscle tension, often it manifests itself in hypervigilance (a person is constantly "on the alert"), obsessive images, hyperactivity, excessive emotionality and fearfulness, night terrors and nightmares, sudden mood swings, outbursts of anger and irritability.

There is an alternative behavior - on the contrary, as if on purpose, a person begins to fall into similar stressful situations in order to experience emotions that have not been experienced in the past again and again and try to experience them now, to complete this vicious circle of fear. Not all the consequences of the events that frighten us pass quickly and without a trace, much develops into psychological traumas with which a person lives for years, and sometimes all his life.

If it is a little anxiety during air travel, or mild anxiety before public speaking, then it is possible to overcome it on your own using various breathing techniques.

 It's another matter when this fear prevents a person from living a full life. For example, a person has a pathological fear of contracting fatal diseases, and that's why he is in constant anxiety.

Or a strong fear of a confined space, and in our time it is impossible to completely avoid them.

It is important for every person to take care of their psychological health. If our body is sick, then we go to doctors to be cured. It is clear that due to a banal rhinitis, no one will run to the ENT, and if it is appendicitis, one cannot do without the surgical intervention of specialists.

So it is with psychological health:

If this fear does not interfere with a person's full life and does not introduce him into a state of chronic anxiety, then you can use the following methods to reduce it, but if this fear disrupts the usual rhythm of a person's life, interferes with his further development, then you cannot do without the help of specialists.

In any case, even if you cope with your fear without involving a psychologist, it is important to share your experiences with a loved one, to speak them out. Fear is difficult to deal with alone. In the famous children's cartoon "A Kitten Called Woof", the kitten is afraid of a thunderstorm in the attic.

The kitten is scared and anxious. And when the puppy invites him to be afraid together, it turns out that this is no longer so scary.

In working with fear, the fact that fear is experienced in contact with someone is of no small importance, even the very likelihood that you can come to someone and trust, tell about your worries and experiences, already reduces the person's stress.

It is most effective when work with fears is nevertheless carried out by a specialist - a psychotherapist, a psychologist with a specialization in this direction. They work leisurely, adjusting to the pace of the client himself, in order to avoid increasing fears.

Whatever fear it is, it is needed for something, it matters to a person. And the first thing they do in working with him is to recognize his right to exist. Fear is a basic, biological, extremely necessary feeling. It is impossible to get rid of it completely. Fear helps us survive, protects us from potentially dangerous situations.

It is important to understand what is behind each particular fear, what is its real cause. When it comes to a specific trauma, it is important for a person to experience the fear that lives in him, anew, but in a safe environment.

Without entering into a struggle then, the individual may experience a flash of anger, despair or powerlessness, and instead of flight, he is left with a feeling of helplessness. All this is complemented, as a rule, by feelings of shame and guilt.

It is important to express this bundle of feelings, while receiving enough support and sympathy. It is necessary to complete the interrupted defensive reactions of fight or flight, and exit from the state of torpor.

In the treatment of such conditions, a lot of attention is paid to physicality. Fear, trauma live in the body, you need to find access to them and help get out. Traumatic symptoms are created not only by an incomplete bodily reaction, but also by an incomplete reaction of the nervous system.

If this is a sudden attack of fear and there are no close people nearby, you can adhere to several rules:

"Ground yourself "

A person must feel his support. They can be not only external, but also internal. Our main support is our legs, what we stand or sit on. The support is better felt when standing. You need to focus on your sensations and feel the surface on which the person is standing, feel the strength that is in the legs and in the rest of the body.

Focus on breathing

Breathe deeply and slowly, the exhalation should be longer than the inhalation. Concentrate your feelings on the movements of the abdomen, you can even put your hand on it and feel how he breathes.

Concretize my bodily sensations:

what I really feel, what sensations I have in my body. If these are not unexpected attacks, but some specific fears, you can try to independently investigate your fear:

Define clearly what kind of fear it is.

Where in the body is this fear felt and what are its manifestations?

The very detailed description of the physical sensation already reduces some of the fear. What exactly is felt in the body, where there is warmth or cold, tingling, tension, some part of the body may not be felt at all. Under what circumstances does this fear increase and what contributes to its reduction.Draw your fear, give it a name.

Try to intensify those bodily manifestations that accompany fear. If this is a tremor in the knees, then increase the tremor in the knees.

Feel what, because of this trembling, you want to do (to approach someone, or, on the contrary, to express aggression).

You can also imagine yourself as a fearful character, such as a spider or a bully. Often a person is afraid of what is in himself.

Overcoming fears is a skill that takes time and patience to master. You won't be able to get rid of your fear in one moment, but if you have read this book, then the first step has been taken and the wheels are set on the right path, it remains only to go

Proven methods of dealing with fear

1. Do not try to deny your fears
As we indicated earlier, fear Is a gift that helps us survive. We can also observe it in animals in dangerous situations. Fortunately, our body warns us of an impending threat. Can you imagine what would happen if you didn't hide when you saw a tiger in the room? Learning to coexist with this emotion is vital. Whatever unpleasant moments we have to endure, we should be grateful to fear.

2. Get yourself better know
Introspection helps improve our comfort level. It allows us to understand how we feel or how we want to be, how to act. There is no need to investigate deeply what the roots of our fear of, for example, of snakes, are. However, understanding the stimuli that trigger our unpleasant emotions can help us develop effective and accurate strategies to counter them.

3. Admit your fear
You are human. Living and acting as if fear does not exist is counterproductive. Feeling fear will not make you weaker or less respected. It doesn't matter if the object of your fear is unusual or confuses you, it is still understandable, and there are people who can support you. Your fear won't go away just because you ignore it. Recognizing fear is the first step towards overcoming it.

4. Rationalize your fears
 The fear of fire is absolutely explainable if we see a fire. However, if every time we light an electric stove, we think about a fire, then we are thinking illogically. Try to deal with your negative thoughts.

You need to think about the likelihood with which any events can occur and act accordingly. This will help get rid of unpleasant cognitive processes.

5. Observe other people fighting fear
There are quite common types of fears - for example, fear of being fired or fear of bloodshed. It doesn't matter that the cause of your fear is atypical: remember that this emotion causes similar feelings for everyone. It only differs in the degree of intensity that you are able to control. It is very helpful to acknowledge that this emotion is natural and to observe how other people deal with it.

6. Improve your self-esteem
Some types of fears, such as fear of communication, are very upsetting to people who experience them. This can negatively affect self-esteem. "I am a loser. "Nobody

wants a weakling like me." Such thoughts are harmful and can provoke cognitive distortions that can significantly poison our lives.

In some cases, these beliefs can lead to deep inner discomfort and, as a result, severe psychological problems. Your fears shouldn't affect your self-esteem. Remember that we are all human and that anyone can feel fear, but we can always find a reasonable solution in any situation.

7. Take care of yourself

Obviously, taking care of your physical and mental health is always beneficial. When we lead a healthy lifestyle (of course, within reasonable limits, it is not worth getting hung up on sports and proper nutrition), we feel great, our efficiency and performance increase. Therefore, when we feel healthy, able to take care of ourselves, the fear of getting sick decreases. Find out how to get started in sports.

8. Don't avoid the object of your fear

If, for fear of flying, we abandon airplanes or, for fear of defeat, lead a mediocre life, we will thereby be setting ourselves barriers. Perhaps the very thought of having to face the object of your fear makes you extremely anxious. It is likely that avoiding fearful situations can help for a while, but ultimately it will only support your fears. You have to face your fears.

9. Try relaxation techniques

When we are paralyzed by fear that we want to escape or hide from, various techniques can be used to stay calm, such as breathing. You can also start counting in your head - until you calm down. In this way, you can reduce the symptoms of fear and distract yourself from negative thoughts.

10. Challenge yourself a little challenge

Defeating fear takes time and constant effort on your part. Try to visualize what you are afraid of first. For example, if you are afraid to play sports, imagine yourself playing with a ball. Visualizing how you successfully carry out actions that scare you can help you feel more confident.

It may be difficult at first, but it will get easier and easier each time. Such exercises are at the heart of exposure therapy. You are gradually shown fear-provoking stimuli until you learn to cope with your emotions. For example, a person who is afraid of a snake might start by looking at a drawing of a small snake, and so on until he is not afraid to be around a real cobra.

11. Don't face your biggest fear directly

It's great that you decide to overcome your fear, but you shouldn't do it too abruptly. The exposure method involves a gradual approach to this goal under the guidance of a specialist. Independent attempts to drastically defeat your fear, for example, grabbing a tarantula with your hand, or going on stage to sing in front of an audience of thousands, can be completely counterproductive and aggravate the situation.

12. Motivate yourself

Consider how you can encourage yourself to overcome your fear. For example, if you are afraid to drive, imagine how great it would be to go on an exciting journey in your own car to an interesting place that you have dreamed of for a long time, without depending on other people. It is difficult to concentrate on this positive thought the moment you drive. However, if we think not about accidents, but about a pleasant vacation, we will distract from negative thoughts.

13. Reward yourself for success

If you are afraid to ride an elevator and are shocked to think that you might be stuck in it, think of a reward for the day you dare to ride the elevator. For example, a bag of your favorite sweets or going to the movies. It is important that you yourself acknowledge your success and want to move on.

14. Track your progress

Keeping a diary of observations is very helpful, especially in situations where you suddenly become discouraged due to fear itself or for some other reason. However, if you look in your diary, read about your successes, it will help you feel a sense of pride and continue to move forward, become even more effective. The path to success is not always smooth, ups and downs are possible. However, persistence and determination will help you achieve great results. Plus, just taking notes can help you let off steam and reduce anxiety.

15. Get the support of loved ones

Even if your friends or loved ones do not share your fear, this feeling is familiar to them. It will make it easier for you to share with them your concerns about being afraid to drive in fog or talking to your boss. It is likely that the people you are talking to have gone through similar experiences and can provide you with valuable advice. However, even their simple support and participation can help you cope with any challenge.

16. Talk to people who share your fear

Find people who are going through the same thing as you, this will help you a lot. If you think your fear is unusual, or if you are embarrassed, feel incomprehensible, or find it difficult to discuss it with someone, try talking to someone who is in the same situation (in person or even on the Internet). This will help you open up, exchange experiences, find out something useful for yourself that did not occur to you yourself.

17. Do not be afraid of criticism

Often, no matter what fear we are trying to overcome - cycling, falling or the fear of speaking English, our steps to overcome these fears can be criticized when we are wrong or we have something wrong. turns out.

We all stumble sometimes. Most likely, others don't think of us as often as we think. And when someone criticizes us, do not pay attention to negative comments - we lose much more by giving up our attempts.

18. Benefit from new technologies
Scientific and technological advances offer tremendous opportunities for us to overcome fear. There are already virtual reality therapies that allow people to face their fears in complete safety. In addition, there are simpler methods - for example, various mobile applications developed for a similar purpose.

In particular, special programs have been created for people suffering from aerophobia (fear of flying). These apps provide flight safety data and offer various exercises to reduce anxiety. Also, programs for children have been developed that allow you to get rid of the fear of the dark with the help of various games and others, for example, helping to overcome the fear of speaking in front of an audience.

19. Filter your sources of information
There is a wealth of information on the Internet that can exacerbate our fears. For example, if you are afraid of disease or terrorist attacks, try not to read this news. The overflow of information can make it difficult to fight our fears and even sometimes force us to make the wrong decisions.

20. Seek professional help when needed
Success in dealing with fear is not always entirely up to us. If you have a phobia that interferes with your normal life, it is recommended that you see an experienced professional, psychologist or psychiatrist.

www.ingramcontent.com/pod-product-compliance
Lightning Source LLC
Chambersburg PA
CBHW080729120726
48001CB00010B/3178